Bradley L. Bodeker

BAR NAPKIN RANTS

by

Bradley L. Bodeker

Introduction

Okay, so here we go, another book of "poetry" or
"ranting" that I thought was important enough to
publish and try to sell it to you like I'm some deep
thinking guru of life.

I'm not. I'm just some guy who spends a lot of time
in his own head. Scribbling thoughts to make sense of
it all. I don't know what to put the category of this
book into. It is more or less observation through my
eyes. Living through cancer, abuse, divorce,
fatherhood, childhood, love, hate, joy, etc.

A "thank you" to my favorite watering hole "Pimo's
bar and grill" for giving me a place to hang my hat
and treating me like family. Fueling my brain with Jack
and Jamie. Lovin me when I needed it, and loving me

when I didn't. Love you both, Joe my braciszek and Renee mia sorella.

Hope you enjoy this piece of my heart. You're holding it in your hand, so that's a start.

Brad "Brownman" Bodeker 2018

People are masochists... they always run away from what they say they want... and embrace what they claim they don't... and the narcissists wait for the crumbs to drop...

When you shatter the illusion, you're left with nothing but broken glass and bleeding knuckles; but that release...

Babysitter...

the diode lit

zippity zap

pop snap

its electrical heartbeat

thudding to life

eye opened

ready to drain

the brain

and change us

to human stains

we connect our

computers

our game systems

our lives and

our kids

sacrificing them

to the televised

god

which preaches

of redneck

gospel

amish mysticism

bachelors

and bachelorettes

karaoke dreamers

and wanna be

hollywood glam

glitz

and commercials

on zits

the babysitter opens

its digital maw

and we gladly

climb in....

brought to you in panavision

smart screen, 3 dimensional

brain death

say good bye

to ambition

nutrition

and pass me the popcorn…

Sometimes those memories...those scars...are just too deep that no amount of writing or drinking will heal them away. That's when you just click "save", take a deep lung and a quarter breath, pet your dog who's been with you through it all, click off the light, and dream of other things..

Love is irrelevant #1

"Let me explain something about split-level homes. The garage is usually tucked under the master bedroom. This is important, because at around 4:35 am I heard/felt the garage door open beneath us.

"Dee?" I shook her.

"Hmmmm?" she said in a tired voice.

"Do you have a roommate?"

"….no. Why?"

"I just heard the garage door open."

"What?"

"Yeah."

"Fuck, you gotta go!"

"What? Why? Who is it?"

"It's my husband!"

"Your what???"

"Hurry!!"

I was trying to get my pants up while she shooed me to the sliding glass door. She opens the sliding door and shoved me out. It was a new home, and the deck hadn't

been built yet. I fell roughly 15 feet with my pants
around my ankles. I laid there making that
 "hurrrrrrrrrrrrrrrrrrrrrr" sound you make when the
wind is knocked from you."

Write you lazy bastard! Don't let up until you've bled
and cried every word you type on that fucking machine!!

And that's the lesson, when you're single and bouncing around from heart to heart at my age; Every woman has already made a promise. Just not to you. Every woman has already given her soul, just not to you. You get the left overs and you pay the ticket for every man before you.

Love is irrelevant #2

I know how this plays out" I said.

She looked at me like all the others did.

"you love me this much because I rescued you. I save women like you from bad relationships and bad marriages. Then when you're back on your feet and get your soul back, you kick my ass to the curb."

She shook her head and tried to hold my hands, but i pulled them away.

"It's okay," I said. "I have white knight syndrome mixed with doormat. I've served my purpose in your life and now it's time for me to find the next unhappy woman and rescue her. That's what I do."

She couldn't argue. I called it. She turned around and walked away.

Love is irrelevant #3

"I stood up, shook the admissions directors'
hand, and walked out to the car. I didn' t want
to go back to Omaha. I didn' t want to go back
into all that dysfunctional bullshit. I wanted
to stay here and make a life for myself here.

But that' s not what happens in real life. In
real life, your mother makes you feel guilty
for wanting to be away from not only her but
from your loving little sister who has been
crying for you since you left. So, really,
it' s best for everyone.

Before I left I dialed Gina' s number. It rang
twice and she picked it up. I wanted to tell
her that I was going back to Omaha. That Shawn
told me they slept together but I' m willing to
let that go. I wanted to tell her that if she
didn' t want me to go, I would skip college and
stay here to be with her.

But I said none of that. When she said
'hello' on the other end, I hung up. I hung
up like a cowardly douche bag. I kissed grandma
and grandpa good-bye, and headed south."

the switch...

i wanted let you know

that i found it

i could never figure out

how you did it

cut the emotion

10 years

20 years

Hell, even 30 years

none of it mattered

to you

but you shut it off

like that

while i lay in misery

you lived your life

as if mine never happened

but that's okay

because i learned the secret too

click click

switched off

you're no longer there

not even a whisper

or an afterthought

i can do it too

i can smile

and live my life

like yours never happened…

Love is irrelevant #4

"So here we were, in the high school gymnasium; Lights splashing on us. Mirror ball putting stars all around us. That's when the slow dance came on. It was "Lady In Red". I asked her if she'd dance a slow one with me but she never answered. She just took my hand and wrapped her arms around me when we got to our spot.

She smelled terrific. It felt great to have her head lying on my chest. I just sang along with the song, reveling in how good it felt to have her this close to me.

She looked up at me, those brown eyes searching mine. Then she looked down at my lips and I moved in and kissed her. It was like lightning hitting me in the chest. I don't know how long we held that first kiss, but it felt like forever."

Do any of us expect to lose a loved one to death or heart break? Fuck no, we're raised on Sesame Street, The Brady Bunch, and Leave it to fucking Beaver! We're lied to for 17-18 years of our young lives and then reality knocks on your door holding a cinder block and an ice pick ready to take that innocent smile off your face.

We were so young then, so stupid. Aimless self-proclaimed superheroes with nothing to save but ourselves. How much whiskey would it take to fly myself from the parapet of the bridge? How many Lexapros would lobotomize your image from my brain? Nobody had an answer for me. So i will look back one last time, say 'good bye' to my loves, and jump.

If...

If you were a spider

I'd want to be wrapped in your cocoon

If you were a snake

Wrapped in your coils

If you were a flower

I'd be the bee

But you are you

And I just want to be

Embraced in your arms

Locked tight about my middle

Don't let me go

Please

Don't let me go

I'm afraid I will fall

And never get back out

Leave me helpless

In your love

Leave me drunk

On your wine

Stay nestled within

Our own dreams

Because I can't wake up

Don't want to

Because reality

Has teeth

And it bites...

Love is irrelevant #5

Everything remains irrelevant.

Perhaps rephrasing such a statement would be a little
more poignant, but in the end, that's everything the
following pages represent. Irrelevancy.

 "The tumor is in the bronchus." when a doctor tells
you this, your mind stops and focuses on trivial
things.

Where does a mind go at this point?

It floats. Like a case of shock, you think of every
cigarette you ever smoked every whiskey you ever drank,
every joint and chemical you ingested in your earlier
years. Then begins the regrets. The women you hurt, the
children you scolded, the chances you passed up. Pretty
soon, they gang up on you like a crowded room and
you're the talk of the party.

When you finally snap yourself back to your doctor's
appointment he's finished everything he needed to say.
He asks you if you have any questions and you have
myriad questions that could last longer than your $30
co-pay.

But you don't voice them. Because they haven't taken
form yet. They will when you get home. When you tell
the girlfriend and she barrages you with well-formed
questions, the ones you should have asked. The only
thing you know at this point is that your PSA is high

and that you're going in for blood work and a CT scan this and next week.

But to you, that's fairly pointless. The doctor said "with this kind of cancer, it doesn't fare well on the treatment end." Didn't he? So really, what's the point?

The two children you brought into this world. That's the point. But for a selfish moment, you can only think of you. That large pool of mud with a sign posted: Mr. Brad's Pity Pool, awaits you. Do you dare wallow there? You test it with your bare toe.

So the first call goes to your mom. You were a mama's boy and sometimes, when things are really bad, she's the only one you can think to tell. At least, be the first in line in a series of calls. She is waiting in line for dementia, and she's getting near the front. She deserves that much.

"Hello, son." She says with that 'finally, a call from my son' voice.

"Hey, ma." Then silence because you're trying to figure out how to say it without crying and upsetting her.

"What's up?" she probes.

"I…." and after that first word, the tears start to drip and you choke on them, "…I have some bad news, ma."

"What's wrong?"

"I…uh…well, I have cancer. Lung cancer, in fact."

Then it's silence on her end.

"Mom?"

"Can I call you back, son?" you know she's on the cusp of tears and when mama cries, it's like Niagara Falls.

"Uh…yeah, okay. You okay, mom?"

A loud wail is cut off by her receiver hanging up.

You let out a sigh as you hang up on your end.

"How did she take it?" the woman claiming to be your soul mate asks.

"Not good….not good. She hung up….think she's crying."

"I told you it was a bad idea to call her." She starts, "she doesn't need to deal with this when she's dealing with her own health problems. What were you thinking?"

"I don't know!" you shout, "I guess I'm just one big fuck up!"

You walk outside and shake a cigarette out of its pack. You think twice about lighting it up because this is

probably what got you in trouble in the first place.
But your lighter works faster than your mind does and
you inhale. Breathe out. And you dial another number.

love is funny. how it goes and comes back to you. sometimes it just never comes back. other times, someone else comes along and passes the time with you, but you never come back to that original spot that you knew eternal bliss. But our memories have a way of tricking us, like when someone dies, we saint them. remember only the good, and block out all of the bad. in a way, I guess this is a good thing...

Love is irrelevant #6

So that's me, the guy in the gurney being
slammed through a myriad of swinging doors.
Outside its October, and unusually warm and
clear. Inside it's the Omaha Methodist
hospital Emergency room. I stare blearily above
me as the fluorescents race past. The guy above
my head is the one who sat with me in the
ambulance who kept a check on my vitals and
kept asking me my name and address and who the
president of the United States was. My friend,
Mindy is at a fast walk beside me on the right
with a worried look on her face. She's pretty
in a tomboyish way, a great writer, and an even
better guitar player. She's dressed up tonight
in her best 80's rocker bitch attire because
she was on a date this evening with her future

ex-husband. To my left is the attending nurse. Peroxide blonde, worn out in her mid-fifties, her lined face, pear-shape, keeping pace with the gurney; she was conversing with the guy above my head and the other paramedic whom I couldn't see at my feet.

"Bradley!" was all I could really concentrate on. It was Mindy holding my hand which seemed like such a foreign part of my own universe. "Bradley, please be okay!"

I was numb, and wish I could have felt something like guilt. Because she was my friend. She was the one that found me. Her and her boyfriend Jason, who was somewhere back there in the lobby or somewhere talking to the Douglas County sheriff's department about this whacked out psycho bastard that his girlfriend knows.

Ah, but that's a world away now. I was heading to my final destination. Operating room number 7. Funny, because 7 is my favorite number. Funny how the universe is, isn't it? I was greeted by two others in white scrubs, female and much younger than the attending nurse.

The room was white and before my eyes could adjust to its sterility, they had moved my carcass from the gurney to the operation table. The overhead lamp beamed into my bloodshot eyes and I could feel its heat.

The back of the table hummed and the next thing I knew I was sitting up. I couldn't see Mindy anymore. A tray table slid in front of me with a baby blue bowl on it, and two giant toothpaste tubes. Were they going to brush my teeth? How nice, and they even strapped a bib on me. If this was a dream, and I was really lying on a beach near the Pacific Ocean, then I was in some weird dental office. Maybe I really should see a shrink?

"Mr. Bodeker," the attending nurse asked. "Can you hear me?"

I nodded. Everyone sounded like they were in a barrel.

"Mr. Bodeker, we're going to need to pump your stomach."

I shook my head.

"We're going to need to get all those pills out of your system."

One of the younger nurses came into view with a long tube about ¾ of an inch in diameter.

"This is going to be uncomfortable and you'll want to vomit when the tube hits the back of your throat." She droned on, "That's your body's natural reaction, but we're going to need to get every pill we can."

"No." I managed to squeak out.

"Now, just relax, Mr. Bodeker." She approached me with the tube.

"No!" I growled through grit teeth, "Why can't you fuckers just let me die?"

"Mr. Bodeker," she put some sort of gel around the tip of the tube. "Just relax and it will be over quicker than you think."

"Fuck that!" I grabbed her hand.

"Let me go!" she said sternly.

"Get that fuckin thing out of my face!" my lips tightened and I turned my face away from her.

"I think we're going to need to strap him." She mentioned to the paramedics.

If this was a movie, they would be paramedic #1 and paramedic #2. They would be played by some upstart actors whom would either become the next Brad Pitt or vanish into celluloid obscurity. Either way, the bastards slid a padded strap across my upper arms and torso and strapped it tight.

The nurse attempted again and I grabbed the lower part of her smock and bunched it up in my fist.

My hands were then put into padded cuffs in front of me and then strapped down to the sides of the table.

"Now you need to cooperate, Mr. Bodeker!" she yelled.

I still wouldn't comply.

She looked up at one of the other nurses, "Can you have Larry come in here?"

Larry? I shouted in my head, Who's this
mysterious Larry that gets a 'named' part in
my movie?? Who the fuck was this guy?

Larry was this brick house that was probably
red headed but was shaved bald. He walked
behind me and then put a padded strap around my
head and tightened it down on my forehead. Then
he came around to the right side of me and
squeezed my cheeks together so my lips would
pooch out.

The tube went in, and just as it hit the back
of my throat, I bit down on it.

"Let it go!" the attending nurse shouted.

I growled my indifference to her through
clenched teeth.

She pulled on the tube and I would release it
until it eventually tore in my mouth and I was
hoping the inertia would send her reeling into
a metal table or something. But she had those
flat pancake feet in those white doc martens
and she only jerked back slightly.

She snipped the end of the tube that was ragged
with teeth marks and reapplied the lubricating
gel on the new tip.

"Get his mouth open!" she ordered Larry.

Larry, though he got a part in this movie with
a name he didn't get a speaking part. That was
my only revenge I could get at him. He crushed
my cheeks again until I had to open my mouth,
and as I did the tube slid in.

So this is what it's like for a woman who gives a man head? Oh my, God!!

The tube made its way into my throat. Larry was holding my jaw open by my chin. I swear to god that nurse enjoyed every inch that she put in me.

Then the vomit came. It was clear at first; I could smell the mix of scotch and bile as I watched it careen down the tube like a water slide. There were the pills I had taken, one by one like roller coaster cars.

The bottle of pills I took was prescription pain pills. They spilled into the little blue tray and I thought at this rate they would need a new tray. I was right. A new tray took the old one's place.

I could feel that damn tube inside of me. It was a dirty feeling of violation. Soon, everything looked blurry through the tears multiplying in my eyes.

When I was able to blink them clear, the attending nurse had one of those toothpaste tubes. She was filling a giant syringe with some kind of black paste. No tube of Crest I had ever seen before.

When the vomit stopped, and I was just dry heaving, she inserted the syringe full of obsidian paste into the open end of the stomach tube. She pressed on the plunger and I watch this black snake crawl up into my mouth and down my throat. Another gag, and then a warm sensation as I passed out into the black.

Sometimes I tell myself

That this is just a dream

That love you feel

The yearning

Is only new love

And will fade into obscurity

And you will no longer

Want and yearn

For me

No longer wish

For my touch

My kiss

Sometimes I tell myself

That the only reason you want me

Is because you can't have me

And when I am yours

You'll tire and bore

Of me

Don't nod your head

I've been through all this before

And if it's true

I wouldn't blame you

I'm nothing

Just another boy

Who maybe

Has something you want

But when you have it

Will you still desire it

More of it

Sometimes I tell myself "yes"

That this is true

But my heart

My bi-polar heart

Says "no"

Turning from stone to heart

Heart to stone

Sometimes...

the night before in dreams...

I can smell you

In the soft autumn breeze

Mixed with spice

And burning flames

I thought I felt your hand

Those finger tips

Stroke the side of my face

Thought I heard you whisper

From those full lips

Into my ear

A shiver went up and down

My spine

I shared a glass of wine

With you somewhere

Within a dream

We spoke of stories

We wrote

Or had in mind

I admired a sketch

You drew on the napkin

It's autumn somewhere

In some city

In some open air café

And two people

Who were supposed to be together

Are enjoying each other's company

Composing their own tale

Painting their own portraits

Breathing each other's breath...

at 6:53am the world is lonely

Cold like a stone. The barrel was rammed into his mouth
and its cold steel rested on his ever quivering tongue.
He cocked the hammer back and contemplated pulling that
trigger, a quick snappy answer to so many problems.
Relief, or rest. what was it he was seeking?

A heart away from bliss, it was out of reach.
Untouchable and he ached to embrace it. It wasn' t
death he wanted, really. It was to be able to rewind
his life like a movie in the old VCR. He would heed
warnings and react to red flags, instead of blindly
listening to torrid lies and leaving his heart open for
pain again. This dreadful thought hammered away at him,
leaving a trail of tears running down the sides of his
face. children. his own children. how would they react.
another statistic. they would be angry and
disappointed. sad, yes, but angered at their father' s
cowardice. the woman, who held his heart would be
saddened and would maybe hurt herself and he' d never
find out how much love there was waiting for him. he
uncocked the hammer and pulled out the barrel of the
gun. His shoulders heaved as his sobbing increased and
he knelt at the side of his bed. life was black,
sometimes, and it bit you and watched you suffer.
things unseen steer your decisions for future agony. he
put the gun in his top sock drawer, and went out into
the kitchen and made his kids breakfast.

Lucid love...

joyous love

found within

delights the soul

and blinds the eyes

how bright the spirit

lost in the labyrinth

of unconsummated unions

lie with me

fly with me

touch the sky with me

hearts thumping

like a bass drum

connected by cosmic

orchestral melodies

my bloodstream hums

and together

we are one song united

a chorus

of blissful golden couplings

yearning appeased

and delicious aftertaste

give me a kiss

lover

make it slow

and feel it

while our tongues tango

breath on neck

i'm yours

and before i'm spent

i awake

the sheets are cold

with forgotten sweat....

Tribes,,,

walking amid

a relentless ocean

of waves of people

some lost and blind

others full of drive and purpose

where do i fall

amongst this sea of flesh and bone

some groups

tightly knit within each other

held by glue of social status

some by misery

others by common goals

or clothing allowances

blackberry flip phone bluetooth

technological status symbol

the cars the clothes the homes

all belong to the same tribal unit

some even swap wives

and dna

at times political wars

break out

and the battlefield

a noisy raucous chatter

between fiber-optic lines

no casualties

except the open debate

war of the sexes

no longer exists

in the open

but secretly take form

of commercial advertisements

racial molds

developed within a written script

blacks marry blacks

and listen to R N B

women are obsessed with fashion

men love football and beer

and stare at bikini clad luster

c'mon,

is this who we really are

can't we think

without some idiot box

or newsprint

telling us how?

can't we parent

without the government and church

social services telling us how?

we eat

we get fat

we drink

we get drunk

we learn

we succeed

we spend

we go broke

we smoke

we die

our tribal minds are weak

leaving out what is out there

more

so much more

culture is dead

in the western world

there is no room

for deviation of the norm

social class

with no class

who's war paint do you wear

on that chiseled face

stretched and loaded

with chemical beauty

open your arms

welcome the unknown

celebrate your holidays

let others celebrate theirs

it's a new world

if we make that way

intertribal relations

throw down the spear

tear down the fortress walls

share a drink

share a loaf of bread

with someone else

there is more to this

beyond the line in the dirt

because after all

that's all we are

dirt....

i will mourn this

like i mourned all the others

and another will come along

and i may feel the same way

or perhaps the roles will switch

but thank you

for the memory of you

something

to put in this painful scrapbook

to dwell and die over

or

perhaps not....

Eternal Yearn...

rangi, sky father

papatua, earth mother

held in embrace

since time began

loving one another

with unrivaled passion

between them

darkness

their children living within

their darkness

yearning for light

Rangi and Papa

not willing to let go

of one another

until the children

gods

ripped them apart

rangi and papa

torn asunder

to let in the light

to begin the dawn of man

and father sky

and earth mother

eternally apart

yearning for one another

and the tears of lost love

drip in the rain...

Stream...

funny how it begins

and where it ends

little events in life

leading to somewhere

sometimes nowhere

some of us drift

follow the current

of fate's cruel hands

end up in rapids of

white water turbulence

or fall off

into torrential soul-crushing

waterfall oblivion

some ride canoes

some in kayaks

some inner-tubes

others swim

naked like babies

take me somewhere

some tangent tributary

somewhere with culture

where the girls stand on the banks

with their pretty little swimsuits

sipping sodas

from hourglass coke bottles

sand in their toes

ray ban's covering those heavy lidded

brown eyes

waiting to drown men

young and old

like sirens in a Greek play

give me music

where everything

is played from the heart

sung from the soul

the words sang

touching us all

in the solarplexis

ripping tears from our eyes

or forcing smiles from our lips

i wanna dance

arms flailing

legs shaking

hips swaying

i want to give the gods and goddesses of
song

my soul

what's left of it

stream...

consciousness...

funny where it begins

and how it ends...

ain't it?

Rhetorical farewell...

if i were to say

"good bye" to you today

what bitterness would you hold

what memory would you keep

that set me apart

from the others

if i were to say

"farewell"

would you kiss me

hold me longer

apologize for the past

or the present

what would you do

if you were to see

the darker side of me

would you run away

with a smile on your face

would you file me away

in the daily police report

if you were to find a note

written in small insecure letters

scrawled with a shaky hand

next to my expired corpse

would you miss the good times

or dwell on the bad

would you attend my funeral

or bury me lonely

i couldn't leave

without saying

one more

"good bye"

...

I hate

Every fucking tear in my eye

Every fucking clench of my fist

Every goddamn ache in my heart

Every excuse

Every reason

Every breath from my lungs

And i just stew in this anger

Baste in this hate

Waiting for a chance

To release it into the universe

And let everyone else

Wonder...

Who made the rain...

A guy can do everything right and still be wrong...

i have seen:

-powerful tornadoes rip apart a bridge like it was made of paper.

-rain rush across the water towards me in sheets and soak my dirty soul

-the tasman and pacific meet each other in a boiling beautiful mix.

-two beautiful girls grow into extraordinary women.

-lightning paint an open sky with purples and whites.

-the desert painted red by the setting sun.

-the life float out of a loved one.

-a baby being born without a father.

-the rumbling applause of an appreciative audience.

-solar flares ripple across a midnight sky and dance with the stars.

-fireflies light up a nocturnal prairie so that you couldn't tell the difference between sky and ground.

-the strongest of people grow into the weakest.

-a best friend turn into a bitter enemy.

-a gathering of past friends turn into my brothers and sisters.

-wonders no man or woman will ever see.

I have seen all this and more, and though my heart may feel empty at times...i think of everything i have witnessed and count each breath i take a gift to take to my grave.

The meaning of life is just to stay alive...there are so many moments of sheer beauty you will miss...moments of utter terror...no one...experiences your life but you...don't miss out on it...

When life hands you lemons...cut the lemon open..squirt life in the eyes and kick it in the crotch...take its money and run....

eyes wide open...

the one i thought

would be there

was gone

the one i thought

would be gone

was there

and that

in itself

explains why

i love who i love

and who doesn't

love in return

why the blind eye

faced the wrong way

the heart beat

for the wrong drum

why i lay here

in what seems

as perpetual sorrow

when true fate

sat upon my lap

but the crust is gone

crumbled from my eyes

and i know my father

and i know my mother

i know my love

and i know who never did

Grief...it's a delicate ballet of holding on and letting go...i hate this goddamn dance...sick of death, and loss, that i sometimes go blind with tears....

I know this may sound like bull shit... but you are made weak so you can become strong... get up... just get the fuck up...

I am a survivor...

i've survived abuse

i've survived drugs

i've survived 2 divorces

i've survived rejection

i've survived high school

i've survived cancer

i've survived jail

i've survived bar room brawls

i've survived broken bones

i've survived the loss of loved ones

i've survived a gun to my face

and a knife to my throat

i've survived every goddamn thing

life has thrown at me

and i would do it again

my only regrets, are the ones i've hurt

along the way

...now, who's ready to LIVE?

we've made it another year

to enjoy another beer

we've kissed a thousand lips

and sailed a thousand ships

but never is a man alone

if he has a broken heart atoned

so lay him deep

for the long dirt sleep

never say a bitter word

because beyond it may be heard

tip your glass or raise your can

and remember i was a whiskey man...

st. patrick's day -bradley bodeker 2018

Does my job define me? Does my race or heritage define me? Does my religion or lack of it define me? Did cancer define me? Does my weight define me? Do my political views define me?

The answer is: NO

What defines me is the kind of friend I am. The will to overcome any goddamn obstacle thrown at me. How i treat others. How i react to how others treat me. Doesn't matter if i can draw, sing, play guitar, act or get awesome grades. What matters is what i leave behind. How i lived my life. The choices i've made and the people i've loved.

*this wonderful bit of advice was given to me by a friend over the phone when i was lying in the hospital recovering from cancer surgery. I was in a dark place. No matter how many friends and family i had at my bedside, those were the words that kicked my ass to move forward. Thanks, David.

Happiness in a glass of ice...

I didn't ask for cancer

But i got it

I didn't ask for divorce

But i got it

I didn't ask to lose loved ones

But i did

But...

I also didn't ask for friends

But i got them

I didn't ask for love

But i got it

I didn't ask for family

But i got it

I didn't ask for second chances

But i got them

So...

Fuck you bitterness

Fuck you gloom

Fuck you desperation

I'm not in my tomb

You know you came home late when your
shoes are still warm from the night before...

things you don't want to hear in a public bathroom:

-"RELEASE THE KRAKEN!"

-"Hey, nice shoes."

-"Oh my god, this is going to hurt."

-"Hey, i don't remember eating corn!"

-"Hey, buddy, ya wanna see something really scary?"

Single life: when you can wake up in the middle of the night and gnaw on the last remaining rib bone in your underwear....

warrior...

cancer

death

divorce

abuse

bullying

racism

adultery

hate

broken bones

homelessness

rejection

none of these words defined me

none of them conquered me

they helped me

they taught me

to stand up

brush myself off

and take on the next battle

how did you earn your eagle feather?

how did you earn your moko?

how did you earn your right to stand there

and breathe the air around you?

lucky...

i have breathed in the salt air

of an island paradise from which i was
born

i have lived across the United States

i have walked the ancient lands

that my ancestors claimed as home

i have felt the love of both my parents

and felt their wrath

i've known the privilege of being a father

the joy of being a friend

i have loved, been loved and been rejected

my heart has broken a million times

i have experienced the rage of violence

the deep sadness of death

i have danced with cancer a time or two

i held the hand of my mother as she
passed on

to the next life...

i have cried when my siblings have left

i have shed tears of joy when they returned

i have shared my life

with so many walks of life

that filled me with empathy for someone

who has lived an entirely different life
than i

i have felt the depthless love

of a soul mate

and the primal urge of a one night stand

i've shed tears and caused tears

for all that it's worth

i am the luckiest man on earth

and for as long as i'm here

i'm hoping the list gets longer

before the book closes and another starts....

In the End.

All the things

You've done

All the things

You are about to do

Mean nothing

In the end...

All the lips you've kissed

All the hearts you broke

All the promises

You've made

Mean nothing

In the end...

All the times

That you danced

All the love

That you've made

All those hugs

And heart to hearts

Mean nothing

In the end....

Eventually....

Everyone leaves

Everyone changes their mind

Everyone walks away

...in the end

You find yourself

In an empty room

Lying in your own filth

Waiting for the blue scrubs

To pack you in a bag

Hoping someone,

In the end,

Will release your soul...

mom (1940-2017)

if you come

on the wings of a butterfly

or the buzz of a dragonfly

please, land softly on my finger

or on the whisper of a breeze

the scent of your perfume

the gentle stroke of your hand

let me hear the comfort of your laugh

perhaps you're just hanging about

or floating above

smiling at your kids

sleeping under your roof

maybe...

you've already journeyed

to the end of the isle

the top of your mountain

the mouth of your river

greeting your loved ones

from long ago

running along a beach

with that gleam in your emerald eyes

and you've already come along

in the deepest night

laying a kiss on each of our cheeks

while we slept

dreaming of the memories of you...

Thunder rumbled

In the thick humid air

Lightning flashed

In the dim morning sky

Something was coming

Or someone was going

Maybe it was both

The clouds parted

Then thickened

Swelling like a mother's belly

Hair stood on end

Energy flickered about

Somewhere....

An old soul passes

A new soul enters

Tears fall

Some of joy

Some in mourning

Birds await

Singing to an uncertain day

I welcome it

What may come

I have the strength

And a smile

Because this

Is my path

Chosen for me...

Life is fucking pain

Day in, day out

But i wouldn't have it any other way...

I live off this shit

If life keeps handing me this shit, I'm going to go visit it's family and do bad things with a baseball bat to them....

The brain is depression's best friend...the heart is its worst enemy...trust your heart...or you'll overthink yourself into a deep pit of despair...and ladders are only so long....

I've been the revenge guy, the mercy guy, the rebound guy, I've even been "the other guy"....i wonder what it would be like to be THE guy?

Life's gonna beat the shit out of you...are you gonna lay there and swallow the blood in your mouth? Or are you going to spit it out and spill some of theirs?

If i am meant to face life alone...

Then i accept the challenge with closed
fists and a smile on my face...

Friends at my six.

I still exist

I'm still kicking

I may cry

I may go silent

But the fight

Is still in me

My heart may break

My health may fail

But I'll still exist

I'll still kick

I might get jaded

Bleed, bruise and scar

But you will never

Keep me down

Back the fuck off

I'm getting back up....

vent...

started with a tear

that fell

like the first

raindrop of spring

then it streamed

down a stubbled face

leaving a trail

cleaned by salted water

you try to pull it in

and you sniff it in

but you've held it back

long enough

and like a flood

they gush from your eyes

blinded by sorrow,

deep stabbing sorrow

but the wind

hits your face

cleaning the regrets

the pain

the depression

and it fills your lungs

with new breath

it fills every iota of your being

you're awake

you're alive

you're new

you shiver with newness

that fresh spring scent

permeates your clothes

a final tear

drips down

the side of your nose

and follows the curve of a smile...

I....part 10

ex husband

ex-boyfriend

ex-lover

ex friend

ex marks the spot

poet

singer

actor

writer

musician

don't tell me what i'm not

friend

brother

father

nephew

cousin

uncle

someone up high

hurt

happy

angry

depressed

manic

and i never ask why

i bleed

i laugh

i cry

i smile

someday i'll die

but i'm a memory to some

i create

i destroy

i heal

i annoy

all with an upturned thumb

Love, the elusive bastard...

ah, love...

i catch you

in the smile of a mother

the ribbing of a sibling

the correction of a father

i catch you

in the eyes of a pet

and the embrace of a child

the tears of a loss

the assurance of a friend

the shake of a hand

the kiss of a grandparent

the laugh of a crowd

the applause of an audience

but where are you

in the kiss of a lover

the touch of a spouse

where are the songs

you inspire

in the hearts of young

foolish artists?

gone, methinks,

hidden in the pages of fairy tales

of myths and legend

where forgotten heroes

tread on the blood of others

for a distressed maiden

you are the beast

that eats the hearts

of aloof dreamers

elusive

with sharp teeth...

...and suddenly, we realize just how short life is...our kids have already grown up, our hair is grey and we're wearing bi focals...weddings, births, deaths, tick away like the numbers on a clock...we sweat the small stuff and realize how much of this precious time we wasted...tick tock tick tock...yeah, if we could all stop the clock...for just an hour...to visit every person who touched our minuscule lives...an hour, hell a day or year...but we can't...so savor that moment you have with your kids, your loved ones, dearest friends, lovers, groups of the human race...let it all sink in, remember this very moment....because someday, we'll forget...now come on...i'm buying whiskey and telling stories...you buy the tacos...

Life is painful...just pick yourself up...dust yourself off...and get your fists ready for the next round...

With love comes heart break, with heart break comes strength...i am lucky enough to have experienced both. Some never have...with this valentine's day i give you all my heart...my wonderful friends and family who have given me their love without question...peace!

My whole life I've been struggling to get to the end, when i suddenly realized: life is not about reaching the end, it's about enjoying the journey there....and man, despite the low low spots, it's been one crazy ride...and I have you all to thank for that! who's up for some churros and patron?

Memories can be one's worst enemy...they come into your head with their partner 'emotions' and begin to pummel you with a baseball bat all the while laughing madly at your sentimental heart

I think the key to survival is to keep your feelings deep. No one really cares how you feel except yourself. Promises are only given by fools who believe in fairy tales, and no matter how much it hurts...laugh like a maniac until you've emptied the room.

I'm not anybody. I'm not famous. I'm not black. I'm not a cop. I'm not white. I'm not Christian. I'm not muslim. I'm not conservative. I'm not liberal. I'm just some guy. Work a simple job. Got a few friends. Survived a mean disease twice. Love my kids. My life matters. To someone. Somewhere.

People in a bar will promise you anything. They put on a show and brotherhood/sisterhood is performed for all to see...but in the end, when it really counts...no one has your back...you're just a clown that believed the fairytale...

I have been running from grief since it met me years ago...sometimes it catches up to me...and it tries to leak out my eyes. But I stuff it in, drown it with whiskey, take care of other people's problems so I never have to face it again...but I can hear it knocking again....

I think most women just like the attention.
They like to be wanted. They will string
along some poor sap until he's close to
death...then they let him go and move on to
the next...

There are so many monsters inside me, that I'm afraid if I let them out...I'll never get them back in...and the damage and the chaos they would wreak upon everyone concerned...

When most men fight, they are just posturing. When women fight, they are out for blood and would probably kill each other if you let them...

Women have this magic switch that shuts off their emotions. I'm sure men do too, but I never dated/married a man so I can only speak from experience. But you could spend months, years, decades together. Sharing every bit of your soul with them...and in a matter of hours...click...you never existed....

Adults are angry because our parents lied to us about adulthood. It's a cruel motherfucker, that never gets better, because in the end, your friends die and you'll die...and it's usually painful and slow...

You would do well to remember...those that cheat, will always cheat...those that abandon you...will always abandon you...it's a lesson really...teaches you to rely on yourself...no one can take care of you like you do...no one can love like you love...it's a mythical expectation...

Love is Irrelevant #7

That's me, 5 years old and I've already bashed in my first head with a baseball bat. Vincent laid there with his head split open next to my peddle car shaped like the bat mobile. Blood pooling around his skull.

We lived in an apartment complex in the Italian neighborhood of Buffalo. Mom managed the apartments and dad worked in a warehouse driving a forklift. Vincent was a bully who lived in the apartment across the hall from us. On a daily basis, he would take my toys from me. If I didn't give them up, he bloodied my nose. He also used to beat his dog and made me watch.

One day, shortly after my birthday, I was driving around the sidewalks in my new peddle car. It was the bat mobile and I was a batman fan. As I patrolled the crime-riddled streets of Gotham, my arch-nemesis Vinnie "the bull" stopped my car.

"Get out!" he said to me.

"No." I said bravely. Not brave, because I think I was ready to pee my bat suit.

"I said get out!" he said again, "Do you want me to punch you in the nose again?"

"This is my birthday present, Vincent, and you can' t drive it."

He pulled my scrawny ass out of the bat mobile and punched me right in the nose. It hurt but he didn' t break it. It bled plenty and I ran into my apartment crying.

When I got inside, dad rocked in his chair and mom was in the kitchen.

"What the hell happened to you?" she asked, but she knew it was something to do with the neighbor kid.

"Vincent took my bat mobile!" I sobbed.

Mom gave me a warm wash cloth to stop the bleeding.

"I don't know why you let that boy beat you up." She says.

"But you said to turn the other cheek?"

"Sometimes, you need to stand up for yourself."

When my nose stopped bleeding and my face was washed, she came out of my bedroom with my Louisville slugger.

"Take this out there and get your car back." She said handing me the bat.

I looked with wide eyes at the bat.

"But…." I said hesitantly, "But, mom, you said…."

I never finished the sentence. Mom reached down and grabbed my dad's belt buckle and slipped his belt off and folded it in half.

"You go out there and you use that bat on him or I will use this belt on you!"

"I don't want to, mom!" I began to cry.

She gave me a quick whack with dad's belt on my thigh, "I'm sick of this! That boy needs to be taught a lesson! Now get out there!"

So I sauntered out the door with my baseball bat. Dragging it behind me as I searched the parking lot for Vince and my car.

I didn't need to look far. He found me. He hit me with my own car. He laughed and then saw I had a bat.

"What are you planning on doing with that?" He asked, and I thought I noticed a hint of fear in his face.

"You need to get out of my car, Vince." I said as sternly as I could.

"Or else what? You going to use the bat on me, batman?"

He laughed hysterically. He thought he was pretty funny.

"Get out!" I said a bit louder.

"Make me!"

"Get out, I said!"

"No."

"Don' t make me do this, Vince."

"Pussy!"

I lifted the bat high above my head and came down as hard as I could. The vibration shook through to my bones. Vincent only sat there in my car in disbelief. A long drip of blood ran down his forehead and along the bridge of his nose.

"What did you do?" he asked with a shaky voice.

"Get out!" I yelled and struck him again.

He began to get up but lost his balance and he fell half way out of the car.

"Get out!" I struck him again.

"Stop." He said quietly as he tried to get himself upright.

"Get out!"

One last thump on his head and he was unconscious.

Both our mothers heard the noise. We were visible from the apartments. They both came running out. His mother almost got ahold of my shirt but my mom grabbed her hair and they both began wrestling with each other.

No one went to jail. Vincent got stitches. I never got bullied by him again.

Many years later, when we moved to Prior Lake, MN; his family were moving to California and they stopped on their way through. He and I were outside playing and he threatened to punch me in the nose again. I looked at him calmly and said, "You can punch and kick me all you want, Vince. But I'll come back at you with a bat. So, you better hope you knock me out so you'll have time to escape."

Who knows where he is now. I do know that we ended up with his dog and he lived a happier abuse free life.

I never grieved my mother...I had her turned to ash, and put in a box and I put her on a shelf to grieve later...I did the same to my dog...they both sit on a shelf...collecting dust...while I hope these tears do the same....

Superman, no consequences...

I have saved so many people

Rescued from abusive relationships

Rescued from addiction

From getting beat up

From foreclosure

From repossession

From despair...

Now who's going to rescue me...because I'm

heading into a deep pit screaming madly

as insanity devours me...

I don't care about consequences

I don't care about the results

I just want to go down with guns blazing

and madness in my eyes....

Love is irrelevant #8

I went downstairs into the family room. I went into my dad's bar and took out a bottle of Canadian Windsor and choked down the first gulp and the rest went down easier.

I cranked the stereo in my bedroom and lit a cigarette. I was shocked at how fast the Windsor was working on me, but considering I haven't drank a drop of alcohol since 1986 I guess I needed to catch up.

A half hour went by and dad banged on my door.

"What?" I spat.

"Your mother's on the phone." He said, "Turn down your stereo or you'll wake your sister!"

I went out and grabbed the downstairs phone.

"Bradley?" I knew that voice, she was drunk.

"What, mom?"

"Are you okay, honey?"

"Yeah, I'm okay. Are you? Where are you?"

"I'm okay, honey, I'm okay."

"Mom, where are you?"

"I'm in St. Paul."

"St. Paul? How the hell did you get to St. Paul?"

"Don't swear at me! Here…here you talk to him…"

My mom handed the phone to some guy I had never heard of.

"Yeah, Brad?"

"Who the FUCK is this?"

"Yeah, it's Mike. Don't worry about your mom, I'm taking care of her."

"I don't know who the fuck you are, get my mother on the phone, douche bag!"

"Your mother isn' t in any shape to talk right now."

"Where are you? I' ll come get her myself!"

"Calm down, Brad. Your mother is fine. She can crash out on my couch and I' ll let her go in the morning. Okay?"

"No not okay! Get her back on the phone!"

I hear him hand the phone to my mom and mom cackling in the background and then takes the phone from 'Mike' .

"What' s the matter, dear?"

"What' s the matter? You' re at some bar in Omaha with some guy I' ve never heard of and you' re drunk off your ass!"

"Don' t get lippy with me! I need you to do me a favor, son."

I gave out a deep sigh, "What?"

"I need you to take care of your little sister, okay?"

"What?"

"I'm going to go back to New Zealand and find myself. I need you to care for your sister, okay? Promise mommy that?"

"No! You're fucking drunk! You're the parent here, you take care of her! I'm so fucking sick of this shit! Both of you!"

I hung up the phone and got into my car in the garage. I popped in "Pink Floyd: the final cut" and started it up. I finished what was left in the bottle and started to write out my suicide note.

But all that stopped when I heard a tapping at my passenger side window.

It was my little sister.

I immediately shut the engine off to my car and put the garage door up to vent out the exhaust.

"Jesus, kid!" I yelled at her, "You could kill yourself! What are you doing in here?"

"Where are you going?" she asked in her little innocent voice.

I sighed deeply, "I'm going for some ice cream. You…you want to come with me?"

"Yeah!"

Let the politicians rant and rave

they won't be there long

let the media twist and turn the facts

you can always shut them off

fight injustices

don't rant about them on social media

let the unpopular opinion go

stare your adversaries in the eye

and accept their differences

while holding on to your own

let your loved ones make mistakes

without judging them harshly

keep your expectations on yourself

let your kids be kids

they'll miss their childhood like you do

always have your friend's back

whether they are right or wrong

complain to your partner

not to the rest the of the world

Do things you're uncomfortable with

keep your power to yourself

never share it or give it away

hug someone when they need it

even when they don't

guard your heart

but give it to the right person

listen to the sound of nature

she speaks to you in her own language

this life is short

i may not be here tomorrow

i may not see the stars tonight

i may never see you again

but if i do, i consider myself lucky

so if there's a day

you no longer see or hear from me

know you were in my thoughts

loving the memories we shared...

Government and religion—

Two things meant to bring mankind

together

Has ripped them apart...

Don't trust the young to know how to love...

They haven't had their hearts broken

enough

To care about breaking yours

I don't need anyone to have my back...

I have my own...always have...

Love is irrelevant #9

That's me, lying in the grass in front of my
house. Liz is lying next to me. I'm acting
aloof to her presence, because I don't want
her to know that I find her attractive. It is
bothering her even more because she's used to
getting the reaction she wants from boys.

She came over on a whim. Mostly because every
girl there has tried to ask me out on a
"date" and I said "no" to all of them.
MaryJo asked me if I was gay. But my sexual
preference had nothing to do with it. It was
because I had my plan, and no one was going to
deter me from it. She took that as a challenge
and showed up at my door step.

So there we were. Lying in the front yard
sharing a box of fortune cookies. Sounds like a

poem or something doesn' t it? But that' s what we did that first day we spent together. Ate fortune cookies and talked about religion. She was Roman Catholic. A strong Roman Catholic. Me? I was a mediocre Methodist.

"Do you believe that God has a plan for all of us?" She asked.

"What do you mean?" I answered with a question.

"You know, like…he' s got someone out there picked out for us to be with."

"Like fate?"

"Kind of. Like a pre-destiny."

"I' m quite certain that is the reader' s digest version of 'fate' , Liz."

She playfully punched me in the arm.

"Think you're so smart, don't you?" she teased.

I shrugged my shoulders and acted indifferent to her touch.

"Okay, okay." I said. "Tell you what. Why don't we each take a fortune cookie and crack it open. Whatever the fortune says, it will be our fate."

Her lips lit with a smile, "Okay."

She pulled out a cookie and handed it to me. She then grabbed one for herself and then cracked it open. She put one half of the cookie into her mouth and then slowly crunched it. Her face was blank.

"What?" I said.

No answer.

"Hello? What does it say?"

She nudged me, "You open yours first. Then I'll tell you."

"Ohhhkayyy."

I cracked mine open and pulled out the thin strip of paper trapped within the folds of the cookie.

"You will find love in the most unlikely of places" It read.

She looked at it with her mouth agape.

"What?" I said, "What does yours say?"

"You are with the one you will spend the rest of your life with."

She stared at me with those green eyes of hers. Her expression of school girl anticipation drove me mad.

"Oh, c'mon." I said eventually, "It's a cookie."

"Brad," she said with a gasp. "It's fate. You and I. We're….we're fate."

I stood up in the grass. I was angry at the gods or goddesses that came up with these words of wisdom and jammed them into a slightly sugary cookie.

"I gotta go in." I finally said.

"I'm coming with you." She insisted.

"Seriously, Liz, I gotta go. I need to be alone."

She followed me in the house anyways. We ended up in my room, on my bed, and she was snuggled up to me. I was losing this battle of wits.

"Do you think you can deny me?" she said playfully, "Do you think you can deny fate?"

"Liz," I said feeling weaker. "C' mon. It was a fuckin' fortune cookie."

Her leg stretched out and then went along my hip. She pulled my head close and breathed into my ear. I think I was shaking at that point.

"Deny me, Brad." She whispered, "Let me see how tough you are."

She then stabbed her tongue into my ear. Suddenly, my zipper was uncomfortable and my will power was shot. Plan? What plan?

I pulled the back of her long brown hair and sucked on those full lips of hers. A small moan came from her throat. We spent three hours like that.

I awoke last night

With your sweat and scent

Glazed on my skin

Beyond the pillow

An empty imprint

That should be your head

Nestled next to mine

Nights are lonely for you

Mornings are lonely for me"

every word

from those lips

like grapes

crushed into wine

mixing with each other

to intoxicate

the sense of smell

the sense of taste

and i swirl your words around

on my parched tongue

letting the wine

sit on my taste buds

absorbing their meaning

and slowly

i'd swallow them down

and remember every last detail....

Love is irrelevant #10

When I got to Omaha, we planned to meet up at her friend's house where she told her parents that she was sleeping over at. I picked her up and we went off to get a hotel room. But the place we planned to stay would only accept credit cards and I had none. I was a starving art student for fuck's sake.

So what did we do? We drove to the park. Camped out in the back of my old man's bronco II. Yeah, the same Bronco II that was going to be mine and Gina's first time. That thought made me hesitate. But why? Why am I hesitating? Jenny said she wanted to wait with me. After 3 years of dating she wanted to wait and I was okay with waiting because I loved her. Then after I moved, she fucked my foster brother

Shannon. What the fuck is that??? Yeah, fuck the sentimental shit. Liz wanted to fuck and I wanted to fuck and we were going to fuck, and "fuck" we did.

That was my first time. That was Liz's first time. It wasn't some romantic fantasy that we all made it out to be as teens. It was rough, sweaty and awkward. Don't get me wrong, it felt great; but that first time, there was no emotion there, just a need.

The sun rips

Through a cloud

Warms the skin

And opens the eye

I see you

Lying next to me

A smile

On your sleeping lips

I can't wait for your eyes

To open and see me

Drowning in that beautiful abyss

That is your stare

The sun warms me

And I you

Don't be afraid

To touch me

I was made for this

And so much more....

Every breath, Every tear

Every laugh, Every moan

I hope it's forever

This thing, This whatever

This love?

I don't know

What it is

Only that

You're the lost puzzle piece

In this thing

I call a life...

Somedays

Are bad

When I can't smile

Anymore

Can't fight

When reality

Catches up

And hits me in the face

With a cinder block

Somedays

Are dark

Cold and hopeless

When I can't

Even pretend

I'm a shallow pool

Of emotional distress

Somedays

I wish I could just quit breathing

But someone

Somewhere

Like a shot of adrenaline

And I brush off the dust

And keep trudging forward

Love is irrelevant #11

That's me, at a funeral for a little kid I
used to babysit with a girl I was friends with
in high school. It was her little brother. But
he wasn't little anymore. He was 21 and for
some reason he had shot himself in the head.

I got the call late at night. I don't know how
Lynne found my phone number but she did.

"Bradley?" the voice was recognizable, but it
was late and I wasn't coherent.

"Yeah?" I said groggily, "Who is this?"

"It' s me, Lynne."

"Who?"

"I know it' s been awhile, but it' s me, Lynne Anderson?"

"Holy shit! Blondie?"

That was her nickname I gave her back in the early 80' s.

"Hahahahaha⋯I haven' t been called that in a very long time."

"What's up? What's happening?"

"I⋯.I just though you should know."

"Know what?"

"It's James. He committed suicide."

"Jesus! James? Your little brother James? Oh my God, honey, I'm so sorry."

"Thanks." She was sobbing now.

"How' s your mom and dad taking it?"

"As you would expect them too."

It was a dumb question, but in situations like this I don' t think anyone knows really what to say.

"Please, send my love to your family, Lynne."

"Can you come?"

"To the funeral? Yes, of course. When is it?"

"In a couple days. We'll be having it in Fair Lakes."

"Yeah, I'll be there."

"Thanks, Bradley, that means a lot to me."

"No worries, hon, I'll be there. I'll book the hotel when I get off the phone with you."

I've always had a bit of a crush on Lynne and I was excited to see her, even under these circumstances. But all that changed when I met her husband and 4 kids.

It was good to see everyone, despite the somber mood of everyone, it was healing to have those from your past comfort one another. I really think that's what it's all about, why we're all here. Support when we really need it.

Her husband and kids weren't very happy to meet me, they had heard Lynne talk about me a lot before I got there. I understood. I don't know how I'd feel if some guy showed up from my wife's past whom she talked about constantly. So, when the funeral was over and the after dinner was done, I went back to my super 8 room and started to retire. But there was a knock at my door.

"Hi, Brad." Lynne said outside my hotel room.

"Hey," I said nervously looking around, "What are you doing here?"

"I just wanted to see you. We barely had time to visit."

"Well, your husband and kids weren' t very warm towards me, so⋯.I thought it best if I kept my distance."

She smiled a bit, "Yeah, you were the topic of conversation all the way home."

"So, you decided it was a good idea to come to my hotel room?"

"I told them I was going to check on my mom."

"Well….um…come in."

She came in and we sat on the bed.

"I'm so sorry, Lynne." I said rubbing her back, "I can't imagine how this feels."

"It's so unfair." She started to sob and I held her into my shoulder.

"It is, Lynne. Just let it out."

"Oh, Brad, I've missed you so much."

Her arms tightened around me.

"I've missed you too."

She looked up at me and caressed my face with her hand.

"It should have been you." She said in a whisper.

"Um···that died?"

"No, silly."

"I guess I don't understand what you mean."

"I should have married you."

I didn't know what to say to that. I just sat there silently staring into her eyes.

She leaned in to kiss me. I kissed her back.

"Lynne," I said when we came up for air. "You're grieving….we…can't do this…"

"Do you remember the pact we made when we were kids?"

"I really don't remember a whole lot from back in the day."

"We said, if we didn't find anyone to marry by the time we were 30, we'd marry each other."

"We did?"

"Bradley, I' ve always loved you."

"Why are you telling me this now??? After your brother' s funeral??? After you got married and had a mess of kids???"

"I was stupid back then."

"Lynne, we were all stupid back then."

"Can I stay the night?"

"Lynne⋯.I want you to⋯but I don't think now is a good time to."

"We can just lay next to each other. We don't have to do anything. You've always made me feel safe. Do you remember? When dad would get violent? You were always there."

"I was your friend, Lynne, of course I'm going to be there."

"Then be there for me tonight. Please?"

I stood up and pulled the blankets back on my bed. She undressed and climbed in. I crawled into the other side after undressing. She curled up next to me and buried her head on my chest and draped her leg across my hip.

I reached over and turned off the light and then put my arm around her.

"I love you, Bradley." She said again.

"I love you too, Lynne." I said into her ear.

"Can you call me 'blondie' again?"

"I love you too···Blondie."

She leaned over and kissed me long and hard.
She felt her way around me and we made love. It
was beautiful.

In the morning, she was gone.

behind the veil

who knows

what life

is like after this one

who knows

what lies beyond

that great gossamer veil

the christians think they know

they write gospels on it

they each have their own version

the JW's and mormons

will bring it to your door

and ram it down your throat

the catholics and their saints

the muslims and their martyrs

the buddhist just watch it happen

the scientists and their theories

the poets and their literal spitting

the philosophers and the anarchaic wisdom

the atheists and their maggot food

every heathenistic one of us

we all arrogantly think we know

what lies behind curtain number 2

but when our bright light

gets blown out

we'll all see

maybe with a small chuckle

maybe a mind shattering scream

or perhaps just a quiet sigh

we'll all see

just how wrong

we all really are....

Love is irrelevant #12

That's me, standing by the popcorn machine at Doc's Bar with my high school friend, Mark. Its ladies' night and we were like most guys at that age, we were looking for crumbs. There were male strippers in the back so when the dancer's had a break we'd move in.

The first break came and out they came from the back room. Out she came. She had long thick curly hair and dark brown eyes. She came walking towards us.

"Holy shit, man." I said nervously, "Lookit this one."

"Dude," Mark said. "She wouldn't give you the time of day."

She came over and excused herself as she went for some popcorn. She scooped up a bowl of popcorn and began to walk away.

"Hey!" I shouted after her.

She turned around.

"That shit ain' t free!"

She walked up to me, handed the popcorn to Mark and laid a long-wet kiss on my mouth. She withdrew and I tried to catch my breath.

"How' s that?" she smiled.

"That⋯uh⋯that will work."

She didn' t return to the backroom. She sat up at the bar and I bought her a drink.

"Brad." I said holding out my hand.

"Suzy." She said and shook my hand.

We danced and made out in the parking lot.
Before I left she asked for my number. I took
off my shirt and wrote it on the sleeve.

"You could' ve just used a napkin." She
laughed.

"This way you have to see me again to return
my shirt." I laughed back.

She called me, and we went out and played pool
at a place called Russ' s Pub. She really
craved love. Maybe that' s not it, maybe she
just craved the affection. Maybe that' s it.
Because at the end of that night she laid
something heavy on me.

"Brad," she started. "Need to make some ground rules before this goes any further."

"Um…okay." This was different.

"First of all, I still love my husband."

Okay, that stung a bit.

"He died about 5 months ago in a canoe accident on the Cannon River."

"Oh, Jesus! Suzy, I'm sorry I--- "

"Let me finish. I'm just looking for something physical. The companionship is nice, but I really just want the physical thing right now. No strings."

"Which means?"

"Well, if you're horny, then call me. If I'm horny, I'll call you. Just no 'I love yous' right now. Okay?"

"That works." I agreed without thinking.

We called each other a lot. There wasn't a free moment we weren't together doing…stuff. We went to dinner, movies, etc. But it always ended with sex and then she sent me on my way when she was happy.

For a while that worked for me. There was no drama and I always got what I came for.

Then I made one very crucial, idiotic, stupid mistake.

It was New Year's Eve. It was a perfect night, we partied with a bunch of her friends. None of us could drive so it was a sleep over. It was the first morning I woke up next to her. She was beautiful, that angelic face lying there in a bed of her thick hair. Her naked body with curves in the right places.

I got up and made breakfast. I put it all on a tray and woke her up.

"Oh my!" she said, "Breakfast in bed?"

"Eggs a la Bradley." I smiled.

"Perfect!"

"I'll be back for one more surprise."

I went out into the living room and grabbed someone's guitar lying against the couch. I went back into her room and began to sing "Suzy Q" to her.

"Suzy Q, baby, I love you···oh Suzy Q!"

"Thank you, Brad, that was beautiful."

"I love you, Suzy." I said in a half whisper.

"What?"

"I said, 'I love you' ." It was a little louder.

"Brad, we talked about this."

"I know, I know we did. But, we've been seeing each other for a while now. I just thought…"

She was silent for a long time. She put the tray of eggs and bacon on my side of the bed.

"Suzy?"

"I can't do this, Bradley." It almost sounded like she was crying.

"I'm sorry. I just…I'm not good with hiding my feelings."

"How long have you felt this way about me?"

"I don't know. Maybe a month?"

"Brad. I'm sorry. I just…I just can't."

"Your husband?"

She just nodded her head in the affirmative.

How do you argue that away? How do you justify feeling angry that she won't let her dead husband go?

You don't. You just tell her you're sorry. You kiss her on the head and walk away.

44.5413 N/ 94.3632 W

We met in a bar

We met on my couch

We met in my bed

We slow danced after hours

To a whiskey soaked song

We made promises

We planned adventures

We talked till past the wee hours of

morning

And now I'm mourning you

the curves of your body

The heat of your breath

The love of your heart

The morning texts

The midnight texts

The phone calls

I guess I should feel grateful

That you chose my heart to break...

But that's the song

Of a rebound guy...

Do you miss the dead?

Or do you just feel guilt for all the time

you wasted

Fighting with them, ignoring them, hating

them...

I never thought I'd be the guy

Who fell into an alcoholic rage

Passed out in a lawn

And wondered what the fuck happened

The next day...

Yet here I am,

Grass in my teeth

Whiskey on my tongue

And friends at a distance...

Love is irrelevant #13

I'll remember this day, for as long as I live.
I worked a part-time shift with the New
Plymouth Police Department covering a full-time
officer on vacation. I got home about 5:30 in
the morning. I was on an adrenaline high from
work so I stayed up until 10 a.m.

Kay didn't say anything to me. She just got up
and left for work without saying a word to me.
I shrugged it off and went off to sleep.

I awoke at 6 p.m., half expecting the smell of
her home cooking. But there was no smell. The
house was silent. Maybe, she worked late. Or
maybe she's at the grocery store. Or went out
for drinks with friends.

But it wasn't any of those. She rolled in about 8pm. She looked as if she had been crying all day, her cheeks were raw. She didn't look at me at all. She just went straight to our room and locked the door.

I knocked a few times.

"Kay?" I said to complete silence.

I marked that one up on the hormones again. I slept on the spare bed.

At 3am she came into the room and woke me up.

"Brad?" she said. She sounded hoarse as if she'd been crying.

"Yeah?" I said groggily, "What's up, honey?"

"I don't want you to be mad at me."

"Why would I be mad at you?"

"I've been doing a lot of thinking. About the baby. About being a parent."

"Me too."

"You don't understand, Brad, I don't think I can do this. In fact, I know I can't do this!"

She began to sob again.

I wrapped my arms around her and kissed her head.

"Shhhh." I whispered, "Honey, it's gonna be okay. We're going to be great parents. You're just getting the jitters. Every parent goes through this."

"I can' t, Brad! I just can' t!" she was hysterical, "I can' t bring a child up, I' m too fucked up in the head!"

"Kay, take it easy. None of us are perfect."

"You' re going to be soooo mad at me! You' re going to hate me!"

"We' re a team, baby."

"I had an abortion."

Silence.

Silence, not because I' m a pro-life advocate. But because that was my child growing inside there. I was going to be its dad. I was going to give it a better childhood than I ever had. The baby was going to cure Kay of her depression. I was going to have someone love me unconditionally.

I got off the bed leaving Kay there sobbing.

"See?" she whined, "I told you, you would hate me!"

"I don' t hate you, Kay." And part of that was a lie. Because right at that moment I hated her so bad I wanted to choke the life from her fucking face.

"You do too! I can tell! I can tell it in your eyes!"

She reached out and wanted me to return to the bed and comfort her. But all I could think about was that little life that never got to meet me. That never got a chance at life because this fucked up piece of shit of a wife killed my fucking kid!

"I'm going to go for a drive." I said coldly.

"Where are you going?" she cried some more.

"I don't know, Kay!" I raised my voice, "I just can't be around you right now! I can't deal with this…this…this crazy! I need to clear my head!"

I look back and am glad I didn't stay. Because several times I looked at my service pistol and thought about putting a hollow point in her fucking head. But I walked out, leaving her a heaping pile of schizoid emotions.

I drove to the police department. I went downstairs into the shooting range and wasted about 6 boxes of ammo. Then I drove to the Golden Valley Park Reserve and walked in the woods until the sun came through the dense branches.

I cried. I cried in anger. I cried in grief. I was angry at God, I was angry at myself, I was angry at Kay. I was angry at life. I busted my knuckles hitting an old cottonwood.

Cancer

The eater of souls

The eater of life

The eater of will

The eater of loved ones

I have fought you twice

I don't know if I can do it again

That last one almost took all the fight from

me

However you creep back into my life...

I'll be waiting for you...

Pour me another drink, motherfucker,

I've got to drown this monster before he

resurfaces...

When you date a bartender

You have to watch a million men grope her

with their eyes

Another million ask her out

And you have to stay silent...

You have to keep smiling...

Doesn't matter if you've lost your past loves

To other men better than you

This is gonna be different......

Hahahahahaha...wake up, fucker, you

ain't that lucky...

June 21

My grandmother died a year ago today...

I woke up this morning and cried...like it

was just yesterday...

I always called my grandma when I was

sad...

Now what?

Love is irrelevant #(who's seriously counting by now?)

That's me. The guy pulling up in his 1982 Monte Carlo. I was excited. It was date night. I was going to wow her. I was going to make her forget about every other guy. I don't care who she dated, she was going to want just me.

But as I pulled up, there was a BMW sitting in her driveway. I pulled up to the curb. I got out of the car when I saw her come out. She was dressed to the nines. Heels, short dress, black. I looked over at the driver of the BMW. He was Arabic. Smiling at her and then turned and frowned at me. His brown skin glistening with sweat.

"Who the hell is this?" I asked her.

She stopped and looked at me in shock, "Oh God, I'm sorry, Brad! I totally forgot."

"Forgot what?"

"I made a date with Rami." She clicked her tongue, shrugged, and then proceeded to get into his car.

"What???" I immediately saw red, "Liz, you made a date with two people at the same time?"

"I said I'm sorry, Brad! Jesus, chill out! Just go home."

"Go ho----! Wait, Rami? You mean art gallery Rami??"

Rami was the owner of the art gallery I showed my work in, in downtown Omaha. He also owned a few restaurants. She introduced us awhile back.

"Brad," she said sternly. "Don't make a big deal out of this. I told you this is what I wanted. Just go home, I'll call you tomorrow."

"Fuck that!" and I lost my shit.

I tried to open Rami's door. He locked it and rolled his window all the way up. I went over to a rock garden she had near the front steps and grabbed a large stone. Rami put his BMW in reverse and tried to back out. I threw the stone into his driver's side window and smashed it. He put on the brakes and I reached into his window and grabbed him by the shirt.

"C'mere, Rami," I shouted. "We're going to have a little talk!"

"Please, Brad." He said in that annoying accent of his, "Let's just talk about this…"

I got him to the ground and sat on his chest pinning his shoulders with my knees.

"Oh, we're going to talk, Rami!" I brought my fist back.

Liz was still in the car screaming at me to leave.

Before I could throw that first punch I thought about how none of this was his fault. He just thought he was going on an innocent date. He didn't know she had scheduled it on the same night she scheduled our date. Here I am, smashing out his window and ready to smash out his teeth. She didn't give HIM promises of a long life together. She hadn't told HIM how he was special and her one and only and then wanted to date other men. Not yet at least.

I stood up. Brushed myself off and then offered him my hand. He looked at me frightened.

"It's okay, man." I said apologetically, "I'm···I'm terribly sorry. I'll···I'll pay for the damage."

He got up and shook himself off and then nodded his head.

"It's okay." He muttered, "Just···just have a good night."

"Yeah, right."

He got back into his car and left. I went to get back into mine and it wouldn't start.

Perfect.

Awesome.

It was 14 miles back to my apartment. I cried all the way back. Halfway wanting to jump into traffic or maybe leap off the I-80 bridge.

Words are the blood

Spilling from my heart

Ink is the blood spilling from this pen

A blood soaked napkin

...what the fuck am I going to do with this?

Ctrl···alt···delete···

Ctrl···alt···delete···

Damn, it doesn't work on real life...

You look down the length of a bar

And you see your future

It makes you sad

Because you've become the furniture...

I run, and dive, and drown

In a deep pool of whiskey

Jack and coke

Jack and coke

A shot of Jameson

And after 9pm...I forget who I am...

Manukuru

I was given the Maori name translated

"broken bird"

The man who gave it to me

Said I was like a bird without a nest

I never understood what that meant

Until I grew up into this life...

We moved around so much growing up

My parents divorced

I divorced twice

Attempted suicide a few times

I date emotionally unavailable women

I have moved like a gypsy in my own adult

life

I am always feeling unsettled

I still have part of my life in boxes

Always afraid to empty that last box...

So yeah...I guess I'm a little broken..

Love is Irrelevant #15

That's me, at North Memorial Hospital. Kristen is giving birth to a baby boy. No, it's not mine. Her boyfriend left her after she got pregnant. So, being the co-dependent white knight that I am, I jumped in to help.

She and I met at a party. She worked at Austin Hearing as well, but on the other end of the building. She was beautiful, dark curly hair, deep blue eyes and long legs up to her neck. But she liked to drink and so did I.

I got a part time job through her at the bar she worked part-time at. I bounced at the door for Paulie's Pub in Chaska. She worked as a waitress.

I moved her in with me, and we shared affection for one another, but most of our affections happened after mass quantities of booze.

I went to the Lamaze classes with her and did all the things a dad would do for his partner and his kid. But they weren' t either. But I could pretend, right?

When she went into labor it was unlike anything they taught us in class.

"Bradley," she said calmly, "I think it' s time."

"What???" I panicked, but grabbed her suitcase and we headed out the door.

"Can we stop at Paulie' s so I can pick up my paycheck?" she asked.

"Seriously?"

"Yeah, I' m okay so far. The contractions are miles apart."

So, we stopped at Paulie's and of course we sat and had a drink. I had a Jack and coke and she had a glass of wine. The whole thing was surreal to me.

We left and started towards the hospital.

"Do you think we can stop at Target and grab a few things?" she asked.

"What the fuck, Kris?" I said incredulously, "You're having a baby??"

"It's okay, we have time."

So, we stopped at Target. I was a basket case by then. When we got to the checkout there was a long line.

"Um," I spoke up. "My friend is in labor does anyone mind if we cut ahead?"

Everyone was gracious and congratulated me. A part of me beamed because deep down, I wanted to be that dad that got congratulated and helped his woman make it to the hospital.

We got back into the car and I punched it.

"Are you about done skippin' around town?" I said sarcastically.

"Yep," she said. "I think my water broke."

"Oh, Jesus Christ!!"

She gave birth to a baby boy. She named him 'Bradlee'. It made me feel odd. Well, the entire thing made me feel odd. There were things I saw a man should probably never see come out of a woman.

The doctor asked me if I wanted to cut the cord. I declined. Then he held up the placenta and I almost fainted.

It was 2 hours of labor and she was ready to shower and head downstairs and have a cig.

She was one crazy broad.

But that would end.

I paid $275 for an open bottle ticket because of her. I bailed her out of jail twice for DUI. All the while, her mom or my friends would babysit "little Bradlee".

The last straw was when I was called by the Eden Prairie police to pick her up. She was

passed out in her car in a bar parking lot. I
let her go out while I watched Ben.

The officer took me aside before letting her
go.

"You love this girl?" he asked.

I thought about it for a while. Did I? We got
along great. The sex was great. I watched a
damn kid pop out of her crotch for fuck sakes!
But was it love? I couldn' t answer that
truthfully.

"Yeah." I said.

"Then let me explain something to you. She
blew a .46 on the Alco sensor."

"Okay."

"A woman her size should be in a coma. Look at her."

Kristen was dancing around the drunk tank like she was at a party.

"Get her into treatment, man." He said, "She's going to kill herself or someone else."

So, the next morning, after breakfast, I sat her down and had a heart to heart.

"Krissy?" I said.

She was tickling Bradlee under his chin making him giggle, "Yeah?"

"We gotta do something about all this drinking."

"What do you mean?"

"We can' t keep doing this. We….or you…us…I don' t know…we have to be better parents."

"You' re not his parent, Brad."

That was kind of a slap to the face, "I…I know, but…."

"Anthony is his dad."

"Well, yeah, but I…."

"You' ve been a great help, Brad. But I think Anthony wants to be part of his life. Part of our lives."

"Um…okay?"

"I brought little Bradlee to see him the other day. We talked and I think we' re going to try and work things out."

"What the fuck?"

"Don' t be mad, Brad. Be happy that little B is going to have a daddy after all. You should be happy for me too."

A day later, Anthony came and picked them both up and left.

Sometimes, I can hear the whisper

Within the wind

The truth in the thunder

The peace in the rain...

But sometimes...

I can hear a little broken boy

Crying in the distance

I ran from him...scares the ever-livin' shit

out of me

There's a crazy lady who lives next door

She drinks with a painkiller chaser

She holds conversations with herself

She's alone...alone and insane

And someday...

I'll be just like her.....

When you laugh maniacally

And tears of sadness stain your cheeks

That's when you know you've made it...

Fools are the rebound who believe it's

"love"...

It's not "love"

It's four months of the greatest sex you've

ever had

With a few promises thrown in

A few "white lies"

To make yourself believe

That the entire thing was real...

November: oh heck, I've got the flu pretty
bad!

December: jeez, I can't seem to shake this flu!

January: oh great, it's pneumonia!

February: I still have pneumonia!

March: oh that's a little better…

April: Nope, it's still there, hitting me hard now.

May: My god, why won't this shit let me go???

June: can't breathe, blacking out…my lung collapsed? There's a lesion on my lung?

July: I'm gonna cut that cancer right out of my lung…

August: when am I going to be able to not feel this pain???

September: I wish I could breathe better, but half a lung is better than none.

October: I'm back to being a little more like myself…

November: I'm feeling better! Woooooo!

December: wait, what do you mean you want to break up?

January: wait, mom has dementia?

February: mom?

March: mom? I'm trying to help you. What do you mean you want me to help you die?

April: I just spent two months with my mom and now you want to break up and have me out of the house?

May: I really like this new town and my new apartment. Wish mom would move in with me.

June: oh no, grandma???? RIP⋯ ☹

July: OMG! MOM!!!!! FUCK!!! RIP⋯ ☹

August: I just can't do life anymore⋯I know, I'll become a work aholic⋯

September: Holy shit! According to my DNA test⋯the man who has raised me, cared for me, loved me...is not my da⋯.

October: happy birthday, mom, but I'm so angry with you!!

December: Learning a new skill! Wooooo!

January: oh fuck, I broke my ankle⋯bad!!! I just wobbles at the end of my leg!!!

⋯I see a pattern here⋯

When the guy you call "brother"

Asks for your gun

When the friend you hardly know

Calls you on a hunch

When neighbors stop by out of the blue

When the people you call "friends"

Whisper that they care

It's time to do something different...

Don't be surprised when you growl enough

hatred and reality...people will walk out of

your life...

Which I guess is better than running out of

your life...right?

Fathers and sons

Every boy needs a father

A father needs a son

They play and wrestle

When the son is older he hates

He fights

He believes the half-truths of the mother

The father is abandoned

And this carries over into his son's adulthood

When the son is sick

The father appears

The mother disappears

The son doesn't know how to accept this love

He only knows that this is the love he always
wanted

Soon the son realizes

That his father has grown old

And he misses the younger version

That wanted to coach his baseball team

That wanted to play basketball with him

The son regrets

The father regrets

And when the mother passes

The son hears the other half truth

And his history is whole

But not without wounds

Re-opened to bleed

Another round of tears

Love is irrelevant #17

That's me, sitting on the front porch of our farmhouse. I've got my 14th cigarette in my hand and Kay is working on her 19th. We both were crying, but I'm mostly just numb.

"You can have the house." She said to me, "I'll move in with my mom and dad."

"Why don't you move in with your boyfriend?" I said bit angrily.

She didn't answer. She only smashed out her cigarette and went to get another from her empty pack. She shook it and then crumpled it up. I offered her one from my pack, which she lit and sucked on it.

"We can go over how we split our stuff up later." She said exhaling, "I don't want much."

"Are we getting lawyers?"

"Hopefully, we can agree on everything so we won't need to. We can just file it and be done. We don't have any children to fight over."

"No thanks to you."

That one stung her. I saw it in her face and it made me feel good to stab her like that.

So we separated. I sat in a large farmhouse and stewed over what had happened. Under my roof, under my nose. The guy she had been seeing, while I was out serving and protecting, was the culligan guy.

In my bitterness, I hooked up with another woman. Lea Littlefeather, she had two children of her own from a previous marriage. As the both of us began to see more and more of each other, I got closer and closer to her daughters.

We had gone camping one weekend we both had off. It rained like a bastard so we ended up staying at my farm. I was going to make breakfast but all the food I had for breakfast was at our campsite we abandoned. So I headed out there while everyone slept.

Kay had come home after I left. She was furious, and kicked everyone out. She was waiting for me when I got back.

"You were sleeping with another woman in our bed??" she growled.

"Um…" I tried not to get angry, "Isn' t that why we' re in the predicament we' re in? Because you were sleeping with your old boyfriend in our bed?"

"I thought we were going to try and work things out, Brad?"

"Are you still seeing your boyfriend?"

"We' re just friends!"

"What fucking ever, Kay!"

"I want a divorce!"

"Oh, don' t like your own medicine?"

"Get a lawyer!"

"Thought we weren' t going to get a lawyer involved?"

"Get a fucking lawyer!"

So $5,000 later: I lose the house, my boat, my dogs,
and 90% of the furniture. I also lost my family.
That' s right. Kay told everyone that I cheated and
that' s why she divorced me. They believed her. I
didn' t bother trying to defend myself, because if they
want to believe that of me, fuck them.

Lea broke it off with me. Too much drama, I' m sure.
Can' t blame her for that one. But it freed me up.

I rented a cottage on the lake. I could fish off the
deck. I still had my truck, and it was right around
this time that I left the Sheriff' s department. So, I
had nothing but time.

I cashed in my pension and took out like 3 credit cards and travelled like a motherfucker . The entire summer.

I will never....

Don't ever start a sentence like that...

typical brain conversation:

me: man, i'm feeling pretty confident today.

brain: i wonder when something is going to pull the rug out from underneath us.

me: omg, shut the hell up and let me feel good for once.

brain: i'm just going on history, man. you know how it is...feel good, someone comes along and kicks us in the goolies.

me: well...then block them next time...you're my brain...you should be on top of this shit.

brain: i prefer to think about writing, playing music, artsy stuff...i don't do the violence thing.

me: i'm seriously going to have you lobotomized.

brain: oh, what? drown me in Jack Daniels again?

me: at least you're quieter when you're drunk.

brain: yes, but how do you think our liver feels about that?

me: i'm done talking to you. seriously...

brain: don't you think it's a little ridiculous to post our conversation on facebook?

me: .....where's that goddamn bottle???

brain: i think it's time the rest of your body and I have an intervention with you.

me: ....

I'm done loving things...they either die or go
away...fuck you, love, your only gift is a
broken heart...

I was the alpha dog...

Now I'm just a drunk in the corner with

cuts inside and out..

There it is...

The urge to run

Fuck you all

I'm out...

If you don't think I'm worth it...

Then I definitely don't think you are...

Love is irrelevant #17

My mother, who suffered through dementia, went
through the fact that her son had cancer
several times that day. She kept asking Jenny
why they were at the hospital. Each time Jenny
told her, she would sob deeply.

Yes, that Jenny. We had found each other again,
and we loved each other again. We were living
in a farm house with her son, when I found out
I had a tumor in my right lung.

Pneumonia that had lasted for months had
collapsed my lung and through a CT scan, found
that it was a tumor.

Here I was, in a hospital in Edina, a violent
storm brewing outside, waiting to have the
tumor removed.

The doctor told me it was possible I could die.
It was around an important blood vessel near my

heart, and if he so much as sneezed, I would
bleed out.

My grandmother comforted me, my aunties were
there and my cousin. A few friends.

The surgery was a success, and I went home a
week and a half later to recover. It was a hard
road, learning to breathe once again. Exercise
that damn lung. Getting over the pain of a
broken rib. I tried oxy, but it turned me into
a zombie, so I just used Tylenol and advil.

But a few months later I was back at work.
Light duty, new duties, but I was working and I
was somebody again.

I think the stress of everything took its toll
on Jenny and I. Because it wasn't long after,
she asked me to move out. I went and spent
three months helping my mom. I thought she
wanted me to help her live comfortable and

longer, but eventually she said she was ready to go.

June, my grandmother died of cancer. It took her fast and I hated that because I had just talked to her the week before and she sounded great.

Three weeks later my mom collapsed while I was visiting her. She ended up in the hospital with a collapsed lung. Then there was a hole in her lung and she needed to be intubated. Then she had a stroke and then the doctor said it was time to make a decision.

I decided it would be best to pull the tube and let mom fight for herself. She did. They pulled it at noon and she fought until 3:30.

Now I'm back home. It's a year later. I've lost another beautiful relationship. I think I was more of a rebound guy to her. I had to put my dog who has seen me through all of this shit in my adult life. She had cancer too.

So this is where I am. I survived cancer twice. I've tried to find love several times. I keep watching others fall in love and others lose in their battle with cancer. What's the point, really? There is no point, I guess. Love is this silly necessity that everyone seems to think we need. Like valentine's cards, and kissing someone at midnight on new year's eve. It's all inventive marketing.

In the end, love is irrelevant. In this day and age, people fall in and out of love, those who feel it the deepest, usually waste it on someone who swims on the shallow end. You can love your kids, love your parents, love your significant others, and even your friends···but they all go away eventually. By choice or by death. We mourn them because we want them to stay, but if you have nothing more to offer, why would they. You, my friend are irrelevant.

Love works like a business...

You may be the big shot or the next best

thing,

She may even call you "her favorite"...

But eventually, there's always someone

better,

Sexier, younger, richer, funnier...

And you, my friend, are redundant...

Just a pile of emotionally washed up trash

Or a rumor to spread around town....

i've been the guy with the gun in my mouth...

i've been the guy with a noose around my neck...

i've swallowed an entire bottle of pills with a bottle of scotch...

i've cut myself open...

i've sat in a car waiting for the fumes to consume me...

there was nothing you could say to me to make me want to live...

i had checked out...

why am i here?

because i have a dad it would destroy if i

was gone

kids who love me despite my faults

friends who would never forgive me if i left

like that

sure, i would be released from the pain...

but i would leave a path of it behind

to the people i love and love me

nothing is ever promised

there are losses throughout life

for some reason, i'm supposed to brush off

the dust

and keep going

and so, because i love you

i will...

"Survival Rates

The five-year survival rate for lung cancer is *54 percent* for cases detected when the disease is still localized (within the lungs). However, only *15 percent* of lung cancer cases are diagnosed at an early stage. "

-American Lung Association

I am that 54% and I am that 15%...

No one knows when you're checking out of this hotel. I know I up those risk factors the moment i put a cigarette in my mouth at age 14. I know I have lived a good life. I have done numerous things and seen amazing sites that

others have not. I have an amazing support
system that is unmatched by any. i know that
there is more love in this world then one can
possibly imagine. I know that I love each and
every one of you since the day we met. i know i
have amazing kids that are growing up to be
amazing people.

so in this time of uncertainty...when we don't
think we know anything...are scared of what's
ahead...what i know is above...and i'm okay
with that.

He took one last long drag of that obligatory
cigarette, blew out a plume of blue smoke. His
whiskey glass sweating beads of regret. There
on the screen were the last words he'd write
for a very long time.
Then he coughed blood into his tissue…
"hey!" he said with a one-sided grin,
"you're back!"

Thank you. You've reached the end of this thing. You hung on to the end. I hope you weren't disappointed, I hope you weren't led astray. This is my mind, scattered and wounded. But I think we all are to some degree. Close the cover, take a breath, and order us both a Jack and Coke. I'll tell you a funny story....

Made in the USA
Lexington, KY
30 July 2018